INVENTION OF THE WHEEL

other books by the author

POETRY
Dawn Visions
Burnt Heart/Ode to the War Dead
This Body of Black Light Gone Through the Diamond
The Desert is the Only Way Out
The Chronicles of Akhira
The Blind Beekeeper
Mars & Beyond
Laughing Buddha Weeping Sufi
Salt Prayers
Ramadan Sonnets
Psalms for the Brokenhearted
I Imagine a Lion
Coattails of the Saint
Abdallah Jones and the Disappearing-Dust Caper
Love is a Letter Burning in a High Wind
The Flame of Transformation Turns to Light
Underwater Galaxies
The Music Space
Cooked Oranges
Through Rose Colored Glasses
Like When You Wave at a Train and the Train Hoots Back at You
In the Realm of Neither
The Fire Eater's Lunchbreak
Millennial Prognostications
You Open a Door and it's a Starry Night
Where Death Goes
Shaking the Quicksilver Pool
The Perfect Orchestra
Sparrow on the Prophet's Tomb
A Maddening Disregard for the Passage of Time
Stretched Out on Amethysts
Invention of the Wheel

THEATER / THE FLOATING LOTUS MAGIC OPERA COMPANY
The Walls Are Running Blood
Bliss Apocalypse

PROSE
Zen Rock Gardening
The Little Book of Zen
Zen Wisdom

INVENTION OF THE WHEEL

POEMS

11/13/06 — 6/10/07

DANIEL ABDAL-HAYY MOORE

The Ecstatic Exchange
2010
Philadelphia

Invention of the Wheel
Copyright © 2010 Daniel Abdal-Hayy Moore
All rights reserved.
Printed in the United States of America

For quotes any longer than those for critical articles and reviews, contact:
The Ecstatic Exchange,
6470 Morris Park Road, Philadelphia, PA 19151-2403
email: abdalhayy@danielmoorepoetry.com

First Edition
ISBN: 978-0-578-06116-0 (paper)
Published by *The Ecstatic Exchange*,
6470 Morris Park Road, Philadelphia, PA 19151-2403

Also available from The Ecstatic Exchange:
Knocking from Inside, poems by Tiel Aisha Ansari

Cover tesselation by Mukhtar Sanders of inspiraldesign.com
Back cover photograph by Malika Moore

DEDICATION

To
Shaykh ibn al-Habib
(and the continuation of the Habibiyya)
Shaykh Bawa Muhaiyuddeen,
all shuyukh of instruction and ma'arifa
and
Baji Tayyaba Khanum
of the unsounded depths

---

*The earth is not bereft
of Light*

CONTENTS

Allah 11
Sassafras and Samothrace 12
The Intolerant Tide 13
Inventions 15
Ar-Rahman 17
The Abyss 18
Not for Long 19
Ancient Jiriziah 22
San Sebastiano 24
Religious Orders 26
Love and the Law 29
I See Myself 30
Invention of the Airplane 31
Twelve and Twenty Rainbows 34
Highest Knowledge 36
At the End of His Life 37
Saga in Five Chapters 39
Time Tries to Go Ahead 47
The Island 49
Invention of the Camel 50
Before the Invention of the Wheel 52
The World 53
Blink of an Eye 55
Eternal Enigmas 57
Getting into Bed 58
Feeder 59
Death Came in Rather Sheepishly 60
Counting to One 64

God's Sunlight   66
Infinite Clarity   68
A Small Bucket   70
We are Made   72
Train Horn   73
Poem Begun Waiting for Car Repair and
    Continued at a Night of Dhikr   74
Poem Before it is Written   75
In Real Time   77
Disturbance on the Pool's Surface   79
"Nasturtium"   81
Darkness   84
The Fact of the Matter   86
Exclamations   89
Clarifying Vision   90
The Mortal Coil   92
Peace be Upon Him   93
Our Own Planet Among Them   97
Short Cosmological Sonata   99
The Knot Done and Undone   101
After I Die   102
Or Even More So!   104
Peacefully Sleeping Reapers   106
The Inventor   108
Would Joy Pervade Us?   110
The Tiniest Rabbi   112
Not Finished but Abandoned   120
Our Children   121
Heartbeat   123
His Reality in All Things   124
Brighter Than Day   125

The Book of Uncommon Beauty   127
Crime Novel   130
Especially and Most Particularly   132
Rippling Race Horse   134
The Metaphysics of Excretion   135
The Barest Handhold   137
Rotation Enough   138
Eventually   139
Memento Mori   141
Too Delirious   143
See!   145
All the Great Historical Figures   147
Man in a Tree   149
Boomerang   151
Deathbed Moment   152

Multiply yourself by zero
   — *Baji Tayyaba Khanum*

ALLAH

He is and is not *not*

We see Him and we

see Him *not*

                                        11/13

SASSAFRAS AND SAMOTHRACE

Sassafras and Samothrace though
close in sound are far apart in sense

One tincture fit for tea one wingéd and
victorious though both not so far on this

planet that in some cosmological category
they might serve a single function say as

human appurtenances human uses human
all-too-human somethings on a

something rock in space along with
Cadillacs and crocodiles or fine

tooth combs and cucumbers equally
categorical as exemplifying earth-life in

any century much less this already
tragic one darker than pitch already

bloodier than many though sadly in a
tight string of such historical jewels of

blood-red anguish and smirched pearls

11/17

THE INTOLERANT TIDE

"The intolerant tide eats away at the

shore of the rockiest coast

and everything's shape is changed either in

fast or slow motion over time"

says the now extremely small arthropod
who was once an investment banker and
wealthy property owner

and now moves lugubriously over stone outcroppings
and hopes for sun

*"It's not enough to want to be free of the past
but also the future as well as the present"*

says either the falling snowflake or the
eternally orbiting solar-held planetary bodies
in their orbs as they make all time

look small and insignificant by the
brooding good looks of their loyal constituency
into and out of galactic presence

*"Having just arrived I now find it suitable
to bid farewell*

*to bridge-span and timetable rosebud and
eruption that go on without us*

*as well as dragonfly and gnat who
barely even knew we were here in the
first place"*

says no one in particular and each of us
buttoned in our bones

God really the only one *here*

really

                                                        11/20

INVENTIONS

The invention of the saw must have
come as a bit of a surprise

What was once a flat piece of metal
was now cutting things in two

The nail may not have been so unusual
but the screw might have raised a few
eyebrows at first until they

invented the screwdriver and everything became
plain as day

Button and buttonhole came as an uncanny
contraption keeping modesty under wraps

While the mirror was no doubt a revelation
and even now seems almost miraculous

reflecting some of the world out of all of the
world back at the beholder who holds it

and less variable than a rushing stream to look
into to fix your hair or adjust a hat just so

The wheel is still brilliant and makes
what now seems so obvious less so if you

think what it must have been like
without it

Suddenly a bit of matter that is shaped to
go on and on indefinitely even
ad infinitum if without obstruction

comes out of whatever it was first made out of
from the things at hand and
presto! A wheelbarrow a
carriage carrying Marie Antoinette and
Louie back to be beheaded

The crowd gathering to watch with
pitchforks in hand while the sharp

blade invented by Monsieur Guillotine
falls at its accelerating pace

                                                              11/22

AR-RAHMAN

There's a moment so tiny it slips between the
raindrops and clock-ticks

as if it were a strand of silk hanging down
or the shadow of some airborne fluff rising up

So tiny and yet it's the way out of life and death
as we know it sitting on this hill

It surrounds the celestial city with its slow-motion
comings and goings as if pewter reflecting a sunbeam

were positioned in such a way as to be
directed to our eyes momentarily blinding us

Yet we could grope our way between the verticals
knowing with utter confidence God's Mercy would

never be depleted as we continuously
head for its horizon almost as if

floating in it
bathed in its

sustaining

11/23

THE ABYSS

When he left he left traces in the air
and everywhere

like little x's even more vivid
than the things themselves

And when he returned a moment later
many of the things now became names

flashing in the air like before but wholly
incarnate or recipient of the

name of itself's inherent power
as if blown directly from God's lips

over the abyss

11/25

NOT FOR LONG

There's a sail or a boat in the shape of an ear
that hears sizzle from the farthest shore

There's a stairway that can't remember if it's
going up or going down so it just remains very still

There's a wisp of smoke in the air that
hurriedly counts its blessings before it disappears

There's a sound that precedes its origin
and is a music turned inside out inside itself
inside a silence turned inside-out outside itself

The outside of a thing lives in one country
the inside of a thing lives in another

I know a gnat somewhere is wondering just
how long it will live and the other gnats snicker and
call it *"the Philosopher"*

A royal princess is acting totally oblivious to her
inevitable death and people snicker and call her
"The Philanderer"

Antiques in a shop line up for inspection before the
broom and mop by full moonlight
when no one's looking

An airplane wonders in mid-flight how it
managed to climb so high and has a
moment of vertigo with everyone sleeping
inside it

An harpist goes onstage to play her
solo and the strings begin playing it
by themselves

At the sacrificial stone a goat puts
forth its neck and exposes its
throat to the knife as if knowingly and
willingly

A fountain at the height of its
arc stops its drops and holds them in space for an hour
to the astonishment of the sleepy gardener

None of these events that I know of
has actually taken place but in this
world of event one miracle or
law of physics is as good as
another

That there's water in abundance and
breathable air as well as
genetic maintenance of the species is quite
miracle enough to *"stagger a quintillion of
infidels"* just like the miracle of a mouse
as Whitman said

And his house still stands on Mickle Street
with his father's bed in the bedroom with
its view out the window onto
the same street
though now full of traffic

and Walt's consciousness stays gazing at the
wonders of the world

He is not here
though we are

but not for long

11/26-27

ANCIENT JIRIZIAH

Ancient Jiriziah is not a place
on any map

but its minarets jut up in spires across the
sky and its alleys of camphor and teak

reek of antediluvian atmospheres

and we somehow remember its light and
rose-tinged shades and long to

return to it and see it at the next
turn in the road

Jiriziah of the flashing doorways

Jiriziah of the interconnected gardens of
begonia and bougainvillea camellia and
rose

until really it might all be in the
coil of rose petals as they

emerge from the bud

a botanical rather than historical or
archeological reality

Dream of return inside the encoiled bud before blooming
and the slaked camels in silhouette resting from their

caravan and a shiver of silver silk through the
marketplace and women's covered forms rushing

through darkening streets? All a

pre-blossoming memory or
interuterine dream?

11/28

SAN SEBASTIANO

San Sebastiano so named after the little Mediterranean
cove of the same name

pulls himself out of his wheelchair to the
windowsill and you just know in these

poems over the years there'll be a miracle or
two along soon

So San Sebastiano with his *de rigueur* angel-black
eyes and tossed salad of black hair

looks out across at his favorite horizon and
sees freighters and yachts freely passing each other

and smiles thinking of the dolphins
especially the one he calls *Rey de los Delfines*

because that one had nosed under him once while out
diving for coral and he'd lost his

way and his breath and suddenly became
paralyzed with fear and whatever else might

so induce paralysis this way and the
dolphin as in the myth had nosed him

forward with incredible force to the
shore and actually pushed him onto the

beach now unconscious for the other two-leggeds to
find and bring back to life

And then the one he calls *Rey de los Delfines* went back to his
pod a bit further south and they

asked him where he'd been and he
clicked and whistled to them that

Oh nowhere really I just saw some especially beautiful
coral and wanted to check it out that's all

and they continued south to delicious herring grounds
the sun dancing on their slick wet backs as they

surfaced in scallops of looping gray-blue flashes above the
smooth dark green cobalt of the waters

                11/29

RELIGIOUS ORDERS

The religious *Order of the Gloriously Shoeless*
eats ten soda crackers on Wednesday and
then multiplies or divides the number for the
rest of the days depending on their number

The religious *Order of the Giraffia* goes to a zoo
and watches giraffes for half an hour
once a week particularly concentrating on
their enormous eyelashes

The sect known by all as *The Vegetable Brotherhood*
adopts a vegetable as its child and
cares for it both in the ground and out for
its entire lifespan without refrigeration

The Wheelers must always be on some
kind of wheeled vehicle except while
eating or eliminating at which time they
have special wheel collars they wear and must
turn their heads to and fro to
simulate rotation

The Watch Smashers are an anarchist group
and if you've anything more than a
drugstore timepiece you might consider
either insurance or a loaded pistol

To *The Song Bird Naturalists* everything must be

sung with or without clothes on
and some achieve a real lifelong knack for
continuous melody and catchy tune

The Automobile Thieves found a passage in some
theological text or other concerning autos and
asceticism and decided then and there to
steal cars drive them twenty miles away from their
original location and
set them on fire

Some of these sects have been recognized by the
Supreme Court in *"Naked Mesa Sitters versus New Mexico"*
while others have run afoul of the law and
their guilty parties have been called
martyrs and even saints and have had their
portraits inscribed on little biscuits and
reverentially eaten

They all recognize a deity of sorts though in
the case of *The Giraffia* their God is silent
except for some ultrasonic vocalizations
only picked up by computers with extremely
sensitive monitors

Others claim their practices come from a
prophet who was an ordinary plumber by
day but by night (in his *"divine velvets"* as they
like to describe them) enters into
another state altogether communicated only by a
steel tuning fork and grunts in Morse Code

Every day a new religious order crops up
and their practitioners claim utter satisfaction
and speaking of factions some have split into
warring camps over whether or not to
wear eye patches in the month of April or
refrain from using the letter "D" during special
holidays

And some blood has been shed over these
matters and the histories of some of these
sects by their bonneted historians look
much like the histories of most everything else
with some cycles of certain figures emerging as
heroic for a time and at other times in
the arc of public opinion appearing as the very
incarnation of evil responsible for all the

troubles of the world

The Thorn Jackets and *The Hoppers The Moonstruck*
and *Eaters of Sunshine* have all so far

avoided controversy

though when their elders go one wonders how
the next generations will arrange to

keep the faith as
nobly as before

12/1

LOVE AND THE LAW

Love ate the corner off the Table of the Law
and swallowed it down with cloud-slickness

And since the rest of the sky was cloudless
it ate the sky —

why not?

Now it's not that love is against The Law
though it often seems so in this rational world

of 4 X 4 = 17

(which it does not)

I SEE MYSELF

I see myself
a pink and naked old man

reflected
curled up in the chromium

knob of the bathtub

INVENTION OF THE AIRPLANE

The invention of the airplane I am now in
though much earlier than this specific one

taking off above the earth's surface and
somehow sailing at a height that still

conforms to its spherical shape but outside its
rocks and mountains yet in a space curved

above them and going both with and against
time just as now traveling back from

England to Philadelphia five hours earlier than
I began on the same day

and landing *O God* safely again the way a
panther's paws for example land one after

another in front of it in normal cadence as it
pads through the bush

is an imagined miracle that actually
materialized after its imagination took off in flight

and with trial and error since we weren't
fitted with wings at birth but had to

somehow attach them to our arms and fall
flat on our faces or worse many times before

getting the knack of free flight the way a
kind of stiff sparrow might with its

wings unflapping but jubilantly frozen out
from its body at the sides gliding like an

airborne cross having gotten up enough
steam to lift off in the first place

with someone in front at the controls or
at least in the middle of the wings looking

forward and staying cool and collected enough to
make that arc above cloud and peak

and come down again with us all inside it
now opening little cellophane packages and

taking out tiny breads or biscuits to
eat with our Worcestershired tomato juice above

the earth *Oh* it all finally and successfully takes flight

and like all such imagined miracles justly refers
back to the divine origin of the imagination itself

Allah the Original Imaginer in each case be it
the lemon-squeezer or the stationary inclined plane

the lightning rod or the very sphere of the planet itself
as well as us on it or in it when it is actually

transparent and aloft living corridors of imagination
love-connected and hate-damaged that link us both to

each other and to ourselves and to every
gnat and tulip in whatever of God's wind

He inclines to blow both with us and against us
in these airborne sweet moments on the way to our

scheduled destinations

12/12

TWELVE AND TWENTY RAINBOWS

The sick child broke into a thousand starlings
his left foot still on the golden railing

A locomotive driver in the night saw
processions of pheasant-headed peasants
in the clouds and blew the whistle
though nothing changed

Ten pregnant women simultaneously saw
in their mind's eye the outcome of their
child's first ten years and their
gorgeous eyes filled with light then shut

An antlered figure from the forest wrapped in thong
hovered above the raw meadow
ablaze with sunrise

For a flash all the stones on
earth turned to diamond

Length and breadth got reduced to a
single dove's white breast feather
drifting in the air

If you are a true beacon your eyes are
visible from the horizon

Information from the stars is etched in the
striations of our bones

A dying man saw the huge elephant first with
one eye then the other
and asked to be *"put aboard"*

A recovering child opened her lips to secure
the twelve and twenty rainbows stretching from here
all the way to Mecca

                                                                             12/15

HIGHEST KNOWLEDGE

If the highest knowledge is the
knowledge that we know nothing

then everything simply has to be
itself in order to be known

we an empty mirror filling infinitely
and if it has no edges it becomes

filled to nothingness and everything
is again just as Allah's willed it

and we might just as well be a flight of partridges
over smoky gorge or silvery river

on its way to a boisterous sea as a
soul scratching its head or beating its

chest with pride for knowledge it
barely possesses and anyway belongs to He Who

Knows rather than we who only reflect
His given rays in as

full display as possible though being
mortal while He and His knowledge are not

as waves lift and surge
hiding what's constantly beneath

12/19

AT THE END OF HIS LIFE

At the end of his life
he put down his pen and died

The mask fell from his face
and it was the same face underneath

The stairway going down turned into
the stairway going up

All his buttons sang a hymn
and the threads of his clothes

plucked their strings like harps

He was no one except that in
being no one he was all

He moved forward slightly
as he fell

There was one more signature
left in him which he

signed with his entire body
each limb perfectly folded

For punctuation there were his eyes
which he closed

On his lips were the rest of the
speeches of the world until

the end of time in reverse now
until spoken by their respective speakers

God had both reeled them all in
and held them all in suspended articulation

until the time would come to
reveal them word for word to the world

A young horse came up to his window
and waited for him to mount

It was the color of the sky
so it could barely be seen as it

crossed unless it dipped down below
the hills or passed before a cloud

Who was he was never completely known
except to himself and His Creator

even after leaving such vivid traces
like crumbs in the fairy tale

Each of us setting down God's pen
given us to write our lives with

Each of us penning the epic that will
win the day and take us home

SAGA IN FIVE CHAPTERS

1

Right here would be a description in fine
detail of an exotic and faraway

city on a plain with wheeling birds in a
blue sky and our hero on his

sleek horse riding seemingly for an
eternity toward it

The poem in an intricate rhyme scheme with
inner rhymes every quarter of a line and
the ends and beginnings of alternate lines also
rhyming in a very *quick / slow quick / slow* meter

that reproduces both the horse's gait as well as the
lounging city on the hill now under

a beating sun

2

Intrigue of course and probable cause and
guilt beyond any doubt pervades a

bit of background history to the poem from

father to son and so on down to our hero

of whom we have an exhaustive description from his
glamorous childhood in court among courtesans

to his downfall and exile due to his love for
one dancing girl in particular to now

on his roan horse making his way toward the
city in hopes that his uncle has secured a

hideaway or some loophole so that as a
youth of exquisite exterior as well as of

royal blood he might live in peace until the
time is ripe to overthrow his corrupt

father's rule and ride triumphantly into his
homeland town and be installed in all

glory in his place

3

Scores of cantos in an even more
intricate rhyme scheme and meter (and

all this in original English not some
easier oriental tongue for example or

Malay which might lend itself more
easily to such hook-and-eye embroidery

describe his beloved's life in the countryside herding
goats with her brothers and how she

grew up to be more beautiful than a
stand of cypress trees as seen from the

banks of a turquoise oasis in late noon
sunlight after trekking for thirsty miles

and how the prince caught sight of her and
his heart was vanquished on the spot and

like Majnun he became crazed with love though
it doesn't necessarily end as tragically nor as

mystically but we don't know that really
and the story has enough tension and

suspense to warrant both cries and
groans tears and impatient demands

But the poem moves deftly enough that
somehow we want both to know and to

not know what happens as our
youth grows to be more beautiful in

daylight than the entire heavens of stars at

night over both her dwelling in expectation and

the city our hero is riding towards in the
first lines of the poem ever closer and

closer but somehow never quite
arriving though his horse be

tiring and the sun be descending over the
palm trees cut out on the horizon like

German *Scherenschnitte* silhouettes

4

Here's where we have an insertion of
epic battles and historical back story

and an almost dizzying genealogical exposition
from great grandfathers who are described not only

in their own detail but also innumerable
subplots and extraneous romances and

betrayals are examined in a curt rhyme scheme
that both reproduces the haste of time as well as

the sound of boot soles on stone and the
crack of rifles in firing squads and the

pockmarking time after time of the killing
wall behind both the guilty and the

innocent throughout history in this region that both
rises heroically and stoically and

falls unmajestically and abjectly into deepest
darkness and rapine only a bit later to

reach again its former glory enough to
engender both our pureblood and pure-

hearted hero with his dashing good looks and our
heroine whose beauty cracks mirrors and

gives our poem an excuse to enter into
realms of pristine innocence so

pure it covers the entire history of
spiritual perfection and echoes the

lives of saints both born and unborn who
by their very nature are wider than

valleys and deeper than canyon gorges filled with
sparkling rubies and carnelians as well as

dark emeralds and topazes and whose earthly
light is nothing compared to the

glories of unseen splendors tasted only

fleetingly by some of the most adept

among seekers no matter what they
profess or practice in this world

and no matter what their inner
accomplishments and tastings may be

our beloved's beauty outshines them
all and that very beauty is in the towering

heart of our hero as he rides onward and
onward intrepidly always onward his eyes burning and his

lithe body wrenched with exhaustion though he
remembers her melodious voice and the bright flash in her

eyes and sits up straight refreshed and renewed for the
further endless legs of his journey ever onward

5

Sadly the manuscript ends here after a
few tantalizing cantos in a rhyme scheme so

complex it can't have been penned by
human hand and so inspired it must have

cost the life of the poet or else he was
conscious of his (or her) efforts and only the

angelic (or possibly demonic) energies drove him
(or her) on to such ecstasies

though of course at this point God is
extolled as the One for Whom all this

history and genealogy and endless equestrian prowess
is for first and last as always and as

this perception reaches our hero's consciousness at
last and he is about to enter the

great jeweled gate of the city to the
sound of distant dog-howls and martial

trumpets and ominous Bedouin drums as well as
whispers coming to him through the air from either

prescient intrigue or disembodied assistants from
celestial realms

the poem suddenly breaks off as it most
resembles the finest music of myriad lutes as well as

the sound of wind through dry cane stalks and
the distant bells of goats reminding him

forever of his beloved's childhood and her
present beauty her anklets of tiny bells and

her songs in the moonlight as they

sat in a window overlooking the valley

those few times they could be together
and the sound also of his horse's hooves finally hitting

the cobblestones of the city

                                                                12/21

TIME TRIES TO GO AHEAD

Time tries to go ahead without us
but we insist on tacking it to our sails

or slipping our bodies into it like
hands into gloves

It would be off enjoying its eternity
leaping across glaciers and using rainbows for

jump ropes

but we keep putting its collar up around our
chins in order to stride into the courtroom

with a hotshot barrister's authority

Time would dice itself and fall in a
shower ahead of us so that yellow and

white deer might leap through it to their
hearts' content like ageless children through

summer sprinklers

but animals are too innocent of time's ravages
until they turn to face into its blast at last and

die

We however insist on tailoring it to a tight fit
so each tick of it etches some crease on us or

wisens us into some kind of sage either
smiling idiotically back at the rest of the

populace or nodding in time to words of
wisdom that seep out of us like amber sap from old trees

Time wants to play openly in the waves where it would
go unnoticed even naked among the breakers

shrugging us off like so many snowflakes on
woolen overcoats

but instead we insist on wearing it like a rubber suit
as we explore reefs or dive into deeper darknesses both

holding onto time for dear life as well as trying ourselves
to swim free of its current with our

breath-steamed face masks and snorkels
watching fine bubbles rise and break at the

surface and sudden fish schools like sideways
clock faces in the dark dart off in

diametrically opposite directions

12/22

THE ISLAND

The island always floated a little out of sight
— the island of perfection —

in the huge sea where maps pinpointed its location
and local sea birds looped over and under above it

and the sun shone directly onto it so it seemed
a dazzling gold and silver pendant in black water

seen furtively from our safe distance here

and few really ventured near to get a
closer look or actually go ashore its

coves and gullies coverts and alleged canyons
some said filled with legendary treasures

but no one carts them away they say
because of the island's blessing

looked after by its great discoverers
wherever they might be in the vast sea

always a little out of sight to us
even on calm days where only a

riffle of whitecaps embroiders the waters

12/27

INVENTION OF THE CAMEL

The invention of the camel was
frosting on the desert's cake

just as the invention of the whale was
to the oceans which were splendid and

magnificent in themselves but when suddenly
whales moved through them they entered

a higher magnitude altogether

Like clouds in the sky were for the earth shining
naked without them whereas

with their fluffy ermines draped around its
rocky shoulders no ball nor opera opening is too

fancy to keep the earth away

So too by the same token the heart is
a perfect vessel for getting blood from

one side of our bodies to the other but the
placement deep within it of the crystalline

palatial gateway and the

secret door to the treasure cave and the
singing inhabitants of the isle of contentment

as well as the arduous ascent up
vertical spiral stairways to God's dustless precincts just

one touch away from where we are now

are as whales to their oceans and
camels to their deserts

Perfection placed by the Divine Hand to
complete the intended picture and

bring it to life fully lit from within
breathing His original Breath

12/29

BEFORE THE INVENTION OF THE WHEEL

Before the invention of the wheel
the earth was flat

Before the invention of the boat
the ocean was immobile

Before the invention of the stars
the night went on forever

Before the invention of the smile
the face was featureless

Before the invention of the pin
everything fell apart

Before the invention of black
colors all ran together

Before the invention of love
we were without arms or legs

Before the invention of time
there was no before before nor after after

Before the invention of creation
one single breath held perfectly still

Before the Self-invention of God
there was no before the Self-invention of God

12/31

THE WORLD

If all the shapes in the world were to
proclaim themselves in the spirit of

devotional usefulness and art and call out or even
whisper to us their functions by God's will

such as a cleft in a tree that might be a perfect
fork for poking seed-holes in the ground say

or a particular stone to wedge with another
making an impregnable wall or stable stairway

and even clouds passing in the sky forming and
reforming to recite the age-old epics of *Nimbus* and *Cirrus*

or rushing water not only providing turbine
power but also singing all the ongoing

songs in the *Fluvial Odes Collection* in
variable currents and liquid refrains of rills and cascades

But the scales on our eyes and ears must fall
to hear and see these divine signs and indications

and their innermost choirs to become apparent to us
to whose repeated choruses our own quavering

voices may join and we then be able to pick up

exactly that perfect bamboo shoot of perfect size

and from it make that particular flute of perfect
pitch to call out into the living spiral of the whole

the underlying harmonies of His
perfect Names

1/4

BLINK OF AN EYE

A tiny little boat the size of an eyelash
filled with tiny little passengers

bobbed on the shore of the eyelid as the
tiny little passengers boarded

It was winter and a full moon cast its
luminous disk on the waters

And voluminous fish gathered under the surface
at the boat's commotion

The skipper was ebony black and the
shipmates from faraway islands

and the passengers now filing along the
microscopic gangplank were ghosts

It was a ship bound for Singapore or as
close to Singapore as possible

though "bound to *Singalong*" might do as
well in this meandering ballad

The hold of this tiny little boat was
filled to capacity

with rare silks and casks of silver
jewels more iridescent than the moonlit crescents

and documents and vellum-bound books
maps of places no one had yet discovered

costly garments encrusted with pearls
hats woven in Mongolian marketplaces

and none of the things were any bigger than
an atom and some were considerably smaller

But they were going to Singapore to sell
and barter for salt more precious than any treasure

It's an old story told better elsewhere by better tellers
the trade of sumptuousness for simplicity

But simplicity without which we'd
curl up and die salt more precious than pearls

whereas with diamond rings or cascading
necklaces we live only as long as God will have us

though both sumptuous and simple are in His hands
so the boat bobbed and the passengers

boarded and the sailors squinted in the
weird wobbling moonlight

and high adventure awaited all of them
until I happened to blink and

washed them all away forever

ETERNAL ENIGMAS

A boat pulls away from the harbor
or is it the harbor pulls away from the boat?

Air flaps around an inert flag
or is it the flag that flaps in the still air?

Murder gets itself committed right before the
man's eyes or does the man commit it?

The earth turns or is it the turning that
comes first and the earth follows?

A twinkle in the sky might be long after
the star's dead as we just now enjoy its light

We love a thing or person with all our hearts
or does that love long precede its object?

Time doesn't seem to be passing
yet my heartbeat tells me so

This poem seems to be getting itself written
where before it didn't even exist

I wonder what the day will bring by Allah
or will what's brought by Allah bring the day?

A tomb is silent
or is silence a tomb?

GETTING INTO BED

I get into bed and the
warmth of my body warms the

bed on the coldest night of the
year but one day

there will be no
warmth in my body and

I'll be elsewhere

                                                         1/17

FEEDER

I wonder if the sparrows wonder
who that ghostly shape inside is
who puts seed in the feeder

They sometimes come in flocks and
flutter around the feeder like
Spanish señoritas batting each other
with fans

They even seem to send a scout if the
feeder's empty to land on a
perch and cheep in at me at the
window to come out and fill it

which I dutifully do when I can
to see them flit to the tree outside
then swoop back to it like iron filings
around a magnet

then suddenly disappear
leaving the feeder

swinging

1/19

DEATH CAME IN RATHER SHEEPISHLY

In memoriam Imran Saithna

Death came in rather sheepishly having just
taken someone quite young and in the

flush of life and sat down in front of me in an
overstuffed chair and took off his shoes showing

two identical feet with actually
thousands of toes and somehow between

each toe I saw Sahara sand-dunes as
if from the air and thick Amazonian

jungle with smoke-centered clearings and
people down below with happy children running naked

and every human environment in between
and death said nothing for a while to let me

get used to his presence and on
such short notice

*"It's not what you think at all really
It's not what anyone thinks*

*The wise regard it as simply another door
on a straightforward trajectory while the*

*stupefied are terrified as if they'd be
leaving something sumptuous for something*

*either blank as paint or as tedious as choir practice
when it's actually inexpressibly engaging in a*

*way no one experiences on this side where you're
sitting now listening to me babble on"*

He crossed his legs and I saw at his
knees sets of wing-like flutterings

that extended backwards through the material
furniture and walls into similar but

distinctly different dimensions

And the falling apart and reconstitution of his
face sometimes like a spring day in the

woods and sometimes like a wintry chill at the
arctic top of the world but in all cases

something both familiar and strange
and then he saw me seeing and for a

moment came behind my seeing so that
I saw things here through death's eyes for a split second

The transparency of interrelated contingencies
The way things come together in a kind of trance

The really drab colors of everything on this side
and our plucking at rainbows

And how young or old is truly only relative with
some of the youngest in years being the oldest

and vice versa and he settled back and
back into the chair through dynasty after

dynasty to Egypt and beyond and I
saw how death was an essential

ingredient to our acceleration onward
and a true disentangling but only at the time

we're called and not at any other which
only makes entanglings greater

as in suicide or its pseudo-glamorous
perhaps slower but self-destructive variants

"The young man from the car-crash" he
said looking up at me and I saw

great golden canyons open and close in his
eyes

*"He was done here and is now on a serious
diplomatic mission having left only*

sweet memories behind him which for a time

makes everyone he left behind want to be

more like him
so he's on two diplomatic missions in fact

there where he can't be seen
and here in his echoing after-effect

where he can"

1/24 (at *Fajr*)

COUNTING TO ONE

Blithely counting on his twenty
fingers and toes he always seems to

forget something some mathematical procedure
though everything's in place for his

anatomical abacus all his limbs intact
(unlike veterans of our horror wars)

both his eyes and ears and nostrils
conveniently doubled for easy division or

multiplication then there's also the pure and
imperfect symmetry of his body though to his

mind and *why not?* It all seems perfectly
symmetrical right down the middle like a

Rorschach test to inspire those dream image
correspondences of moose antlers or dragon father

getting offed or mother an overpowering cloud in the soap
operas embedded in our physiologies

Greek dramas like it or not in the
bones and sinews of our beings

He begins with one of which he's one and

proceeds to further integers though somehow

one always predominates as well it
should reflecting He Who made Unity in

Multiplicity and though we might
count to the billions and beyond somehow

one still supersedes and sums up and
reduces to in every case the shining

and resplendent One like a dawn under a
suspension bridge where sky is

crisp blue and the waters below as dark as
thought through which each story has its

end and beginning each sentence of us
fitting into the one story with all its

terror and glory all its sad beginnings and
slap-happy endings so that we

always end up having counted it all out
on breaths and eye blinks from one

eternity to another in our singular
and multifarious earthly existences

that get us ready for the one grave
that will catapult us home

GOD'S SUNLIGHT

Beauty has a way of sinking into
everything we do like a time-lapse
photograph of dark flowers blossoming out of
everything

White horses on a hillside in the rain
couldn't be more beautiful
and the silvery rain itself whose lateral beads
the wind jangles

Our oceans are as wide as the five oceans themselves
as they lick the continents' edges over and
over each millennium and yet
the land transpires

And then there's sky with its galactic
twinklings in a kind of cotton fuzz of
light embedding them in deep space

Our eyes could be trained to see only the
beauty that there is when we see through the
rest to the actual incandescent core of things

Those white horses of the second stanza have
hardly moved but now suddenly
raise their heads and run together
as if the rain were riders or whips
urging them on

And so is our own beauty dormant until
roused and washed in God's sunlight

and like the wet flanks of those horses
ripples with the musculature of joy

2/8

INFINITE CLARITY

Five nights have gone by and not one owl of
poetry has hooted to me out of its tree

Three moths fly in the room from flitter to flitter
their universes perfect within themselves
looking out through tiny cockpit eyes
to navigate from one light to another
one darkness to another

Twenty-foot crocodiles slither across delta mud
sometimes leaving perfect imprints of their crocodiliac forms
down to perfectly printed toes and each perfectly plated scale

Moonlight slips quietly into a glass on a windowsill
reflected in the liquid glisten in a flashing eye and even
two flashing eyes at once
or a puddle of piss a dog's left next to a bush
or a zillion or so other earthly reflections

Yet the moon remains pure in itself wherever it
lands always the same white disc throughout its
unfazed variations

It's all in the rhythm and phrasing that this
multitudinous world gets played out in discrete jerks and pauses
exclamations and praises
which makes its natural condition more like
a single song than a single silence

I'm sitting on my bed and a beige moth keeps
landing or flittering above my two black pillows

Where will we go O God that we can't
see now but You see with
infinite clarity?

And Your pure moonlight lands on
with absolute reflectivity?

2/13

A SMALL BUCKET

A small bucket
the size of a tiny locket
contains this world

worn round the neck of a beloved
friend and stars glitter inside it
and galaxies float within it

and a gnat's eye-size dot there
that's us
with all our wars and peaces

deep inside a microscopic bucket
with a few other worlds besides
worn round the neck of a beloved

friend on a sunny day on a
mountainside with bleating goats
and hay bales in the shapes of
moons

and it all goes on without us
and someone leans across and shadows
the surface of the bucket for a moment
so it all becomes dark
then suddenly light

and we think of good and bad

when it's really neither

in a bucket the size of a
locket

with no curse upon it

                                                2/16

WE ARE MADE

We are made of crystal

and we live as long as that crystal is

illumined or longing to be illumined

And when the light goes out

or we let it go out

we live no longer

2/20

TRAIN HORN

Do all cities come with a
forlorn train horn in the distance
at 4:45 in the morning?

The same note the world over?

The heart a bridge over
turbulent water

Some sky gets under

2/22

POEM BEGUN WAITING FOR CAR REPAIR AND CONTINUED AT A NIGHT OF DHIKR

The small rabbit took one look at the tall moose
and skittered into the grass

The tall moose glimpsed the cliff and knew
it couldn't fly

The schist in the cliff-face reflected the lake below
and knew it couldn't flow

The young mouse saw all this and
shivered in its hole

though no breeze blew as the blue sky
flew overhead
like a flock of buzzards hungry for lunch

But its hunch was to stay low and look high
and the higher it looked and the lower it went
the bluer the sky became until silver took it over

and God's Voice shook across it in a
thunderous and silvery whisper

2/22

POEM BEFORE IT IS WRITTEN

Before this poem comes into being or rather
in real time *just* as it's coming into being

it already exists though in no perceptible form
nor even knowable to us though many such

poems might already exist that are far more
epic or supple or full of perfect lines of

cypress trees leading to a fountain whose
rainbow colored spouts intertwine in a

braid that reaches up to heaven in whose
rhythms choirs out of normal earshot can be heard

And before the tips of spray reach the lower
heavenly edges no voices were audible to us

and translating them into sound and meaning is the
poem's duty like a needle hitting vinyl grooves or

lasers reading digital codes
out of the surrounding silences that

not only stretch in all Sahara-like directions but are
intermixed in an echoing way with all the

various strands of physical sound possible to our

ears and our deeper heart's ears

those organs God's created specially to hear these
otherwise unreachable dimensions

and where in the uncreated it existed before
it doesn't have resonant pulse until now

in your own ears or under your eyes' or
blind fingertips' recognitions

2/23

IN REAL TIME

In real time
an egg hatches first with hairline cracks
then out squirms an alligator

In unreal time everything moves backwards
and ghostly galleons with skeleton crew
sail across a full moon like shadow
hands making figures of ghostly galleons
and so on but in reverse

While in real time a new person is
conceived in an unlit room upstairs
much like reserving a limousine in
advance for an opening that won't
take place for months but is truly a
monumental affair

While in unreal time a foot ventures
out past the electrical boundary into a
forest where it is rumored the Golem
lives and dines on mortal clay

But though in the writing of this poem
waiting for the sun to clear the horizon enough to
make up a missed Dawn Prayer
some have slipped out of time and others have slipped in

great elephants in Kenya have moved on in a ladylike

herd after ascertaining the inclusion of the
missing elephant baby name known only to them

a great symphonic composition was conceived in
Austria and the first black notes put down on those
horizontal staves like footprints stepping into sound
on unearthly tracks

a vaccine for some obscure disease was
actually discovered a zillion insects
(no more far more) have flown into being and
the air is filled with their wings

and these are only the good things that have
happened since I started writing this poem
including things too abominable to mention

elbow to elbow with such good things all in the
real and unreal clicks of a time that

only exits with Allah anyway

each extending feeler and passing thought known by

Him alone in His Majesterial embassy

2/26

DISTURBANCE ON THE POOL'S SURFACE

Disturbance on the pool's surface
may help us to plunge deeper

though a blow on the head with a
board for example can't be called necessarily

an aid to illumination unless it's one of
those lovingly carved cherry wood cudgels

Japanese Zen Masters use to correct their
students' crookedness

But a sudden loss of flooring or a
ceiling opening suddenly to the sky

could be the very thing that lets the soul
fly free in a giant V-Formation of its

own to the warm south of God's love and
the tropics ever softly blowing of love of God

the lack of which freezes the pool's
surface over to a Narcissistic mirror in which

even if we draw back from direct reflection
we only see ourselves everywhere

and that hard surface cracks in its brittleness

and could give way under those laughing children's

feet as they try to cross its icy gallery
plunging not to illumination but to

a chill without respite under a
surface now no positive disturbance can

reach through
to rescue

3/4

"NASTURTIUM"

"Nasturtium" is a word whose beauty almost
exceeds the thing it designates

while the word *"skyscraper"* has always seemed to me
more beautiful than its thing

"Blimp" on the other hand betrays that
lofty floating leisurely-paced air lozenge
I always associate with bright blue
Saturday skies but whose word stops
short too quickly and seems more
suitable to a wart or a
square-toed shoe

"Lavender" is lovely and *"picket fence"*
almost exactly reproduces what it is

"Stallion" nicely seems to match that
glorious beast with that other kingly
animal at the end

And *"Button"* is always appropriately silly and
small-sized so that whenever it's used for
something other than that thing that
closes shirts or jackets that thing is also
somewhat silly and a bit petite

"Tongue" and *"lung"* seem related in their

one syllable sibling-hood and reflect
their mutual necessity in the formation of
spoken words at all without which they'd
stay silent and be read or thought only
inwardly on page or mental screen

And ultimately the world *"body"* is totally
inadequate in no way indicating this
central thing each of us is
at the very hub of creation
but *"body"* is a word too casual to
stand for what it is and seems more
suitable to a cute pet with a
bow around its neck

We call out and things resonate in our
speech

From very high windows even
meanings float down

No patch or atom no matter how
patchy or atomic escapes our need and
miraculous ability to name however
arbitrary it may seem in its origin such as
why a *"tree"* is so called that at
least evokes the central trunk in its
vertical simplicity

We've been blessed by names and bestow
by our naming adequate or inadequate

blessings as well

And a bridge of light over black water into
a silver reality breathlessly beyond our
ability to name it may even be

a more substantial thing to walk out on
than the thing itself and *praise*
(in itself a musical word ending in a
respectful sizzle) our most

natural verbal activity befitting He Who
gave us these words in the first place

He Whose Light never wanes and
Whose wisdom is never depleted

He Who is greater than the very
Name He's given us to

call Him by and the incessant repetition of Whose Name
soothes the heart the way a

cat is soothed and purrs
contentedly

3/5

DARKNESS

Clocks turn ahead one hour
but darkness is just as dark

Darkness after all is timeless
Darkness doesn't polish its shoes

Whoever's been left in the dark
stands ghostly in the mist

Shades and shadows blend together
Just one voice cracks the darkness

Every darkness has some light in it
Every light has some dark

The eye alone sees independently
in both directions as God enters it

Then the dome of darkness slides off
and we see worlds we hadn't seen before

Hidden behind the net of stars
or circulating in the darkness between them

From a darkness that's not dark we come
To a darkness that's not dark we go

Everything's wrapped in darkness' arms
the loving arms of deep darkness

Even as the clock's fixed an hour forward
and the sun comes up an hour late

creatures know what time it is
So far the birds are still silent

as the sky's darkness gives way to daylight
and I turn back to sleep before anyone knows it

and trees await the orders of the day
to continue their silent vigils

                                                            3/11

THE FACT OF THE MATTER

The fact of the matter is that there's
no fact and no matter

Waves of light across corrugated panes of space
each scallop of which cups rainbows and
other dazzling prismatic distractions

such as wars poverty venality office furniture
romance gone sour romance rekindled
all the various snake-holes and zigzag
courses we travel to go from A to B

never forgetting if we're lucky the purpose of this
extended quest for the meaningful glance of
each moment of it that tells us

who we are as crystal facets which by their
reflective luster show us our ephemerality

and His Absolute Light

Mountains of cities have come before us
and mountains of cities will come after us

each somehow operating under the delusion of
self-propulsion and each to each contributing
to that mutual shadow-show

when giant bridges in the Unseen are constantly
swinging into place
and depositing us where we need to be

in a lovely dome covered with flowers
in gardens of various winding ways

though what we may see with our sensual eyes is
obstructive girders and iron walls and even the
starry placards of open space itself

Heartbeat by heartbeat proclaim to us our
limitations and our escape

But no step without its echo preceding it
leads us in no direction that as it
takes place in real time has not been
pre-ordained

taking me to you and you to the
roaring lion-filled jungles of night

where a certain dance takes place among

atoms in their combinations and re-
combinations that looks like the fact and matter of

this world but is really a screen for the
next

Oh glorious ones in our vulnerable pulses

*each life on earth as precious as
Paradise*

each one a torch for another

and the doorway wide enough for all!

3/13

EXCLAMATIONS

"A little shirt music!" sings the neck
"A little snake dance!" sings the feet

"A little boot clang" sings the roadway
"No moon tonight" sings the sky

"A little death pizza!" sings the jailer
"A little pigeon stutter" sings the Rialto Bridge

"More slanted shadows" sings the Velázquez
"Let the worms rejoice" sings the river trout
(leaping onto a plate precooked)

"A little piece of blue flake!" sings the eye patch
"A little grand entrance please" sings the dowager

"A little shred of decency" sings the lost tailor
"A little boat, and hurry!" sings the capsized captain

"A little of this goes a long way!" sings the sleepy poet
"Only God can make a tree!"

3/16

CLARIFYING VISION

An alchemist looks at his laboratory and sees
penguins drinking tea

He looks again and sees it's his beakers bubbling

A king looks out at his courtiers and sees them
hurling stones

He looks again and sees it's their tongues moving

An aerialist looks down and sees empty space
sliced in two

He looks again and sees it's his tightrope quivering

If we look out on the world we might see its
bison heaving together in steaming herds

heading perilously near sheer cliffs

But if we look again it may be a summer
fireworks seen in the distance over picnickers
or the soft chiming of bells played solemnly by enrobed
eighth graders raising and lowering their brassy glints

The plot thickens and thins congeals and bubbles up
and then when it seems to get its thorniest and knottiest
dissipates into vapor and we see that the gummy substance of it

was simply its lovely symmetry or the way two abstract
planes of it intersected then pulled away into thin air

I look at this page and I'm at Alamogordo
watching an A-bomb test shielding my eyes as the
universe showers up into nothingness

Gaze at the walls and see giraffes in wallpaper droves
galloping from right to left in a continuous
scissoring screen loping tall yellow against blue sky

See the hearts of us all like precious orchids in jars
at an exhibition tended by a hooded figure
enveloped in halo calling each of our
names by their secret Arabic meanings
under a hushed heaven

And it's the Prophet Muhammad peace be upon him
moving among us
soothing our bruises and strengthening the
delicate but stalwart nature of our stems

Who sees only God

3/17

THE MORTAL COIL

The merchandise on display rolls away from us
on the roiling rondure of the globe

and goes under a cloud of eternal inaccessibility
in the nature of the world

Elvis' bedroom left exactly as it was
has an eerie feeling because Elvis has
definitely left the building at Graceland

Why have we been created with an echo
that's emitted each time our shoe-soles
hit pavement

as our words meander among trees looking
for a romantic encounter?

Our bridges span waterways but do we
ever really get to the other side here
among the cycles of the sun?

We bid farewell as we use the world
to build a tree house under us in the air

though we fly hungry to yonder perch
and preen ourselves at the slightest itch

3/23

PEACE BE UPON HIM

Peace be upon him who appeared among us in this
world covered in dust a shining light

*A speck of that same light is in all of us needing
only His bellows to blow it brighter*

Peace be upon him who in his time of innocence
was the focal point of miracles that happened
around him

*We don't see with our eyes angels crowding the air
stopping calamities and nudging us down the
road*

Peace be upon him who as a youth displayed
unusual modesty at all times

*When we see such qualities today we're
moved to an inordinate degree by their
uniqueness*

Peace be upon him who in assuming manhood
with all the manly virtues quietly held to
Abraham's innermost characteristics

*A something that takes place in that almost
indefinable interior that shapes us in a direction
of illumination or circular complexity*

Peace be upon him in whose resonance things took
a natural shape always impeccably and
always honorably as if by a magnetic dial

*How we get blown by winds out of our control
and try to cross our river by changing horses
a hundred times in midstream*

I enter the sacred precincts of Sayyedina Muhammad
as if entering a jade palace with golden sunlight
filtering green through its translucent walls

I know where the road will end but want to
loiter at its various turns to better see his
beloved face elusive but sure in this world
beckoning us from the next

I remember him forward from what
little I knew of him before this moment
and he peace be upon him is not
lacking in anything

Each of us might write this ode the
closer to get to him

*I open the door wide and call on us all
to be included in the waves of its failed locutions*

Peace be upon his hands that strapped
camel caravans together and washed his children by Khadijah
with sweet fatherly affection and delicate care

Peace be upon his arms that lifted the obsidian stone
from the four-corners-held cloth and
placed it in the Kaba's wall with the
astonished approval of his tribesmen

Peace be upon his shoulders upon which he
placed a warrior's armor to face
Allah's foes in battle and never faltered

Peace be upon his heart like our cosmos itself
with its pure and spacious planetary motions

Peace be upon his loins from which sprang
blessed offspring of children and grandchildren
to continue the Divine Vision unabated

Peace be upon his feet whose sandals illuminate the
earth under our feet for all time to come

Peace be upon his noble neck that most often
bent to listen and remained eternally bowed in submission to
Allah

Peace be upon his forehead like a clear lake and like
a flight of egrets reflected across it with its occasional
throbbing vein of fierce determination

Peace be upon his eyes which saw farther than the
sundown wall of *Asr* and closer than our innermost secrets

Peace be upon his mouth with perfect

lips curved like an archer's bow and from whose
tongue came all the words needed for us to
live past death and thrive in the Resurrection

Peace be upon the praised and praiseworthy one
Muhammad without whom we'd still be a walking
shadow in the illusory world of shadows

And from whose deepest indications
we enter the world of light

3/28

OUR OWN PLANET AMONG THEM

Henry was certain he'd seen the skyscraper
the first time through
and he plodded from street to street with his
head craned high hoping to find it

How could you lose a skyscraper?

Landrell counted the sheep a hundred
times on that mountainside in the moonlight
each time getting a different number
thinking he was either missing one or
one was mysteriously being added to the
sleeping flock somehow without him knowing

Henrietta (no relation to the Henry above) peered
intently into the aquarium that filled one
wall and counted the tiny zebra fish
as they scurried through the bubbling water

The anthropologist Miguel on the harsh mountainside
squinted in the heat at the artifacts
arranged to form a semblance of the
original and thought sure the nose had
been there an hour before

But no
now no nose could be seen in that
brutal post-deluvian shimmer

Things added and subtracted to us
daily or nocturnally as worlds come close and
sometimes kaleidoscope inside one another
though for our sanity's sake we're led to
believe what we see
as planetoids
skitter and stream through the stars

Our own planet among them

3/30

SHORT COSMOLOGICAL SONATA

An owl flew past and told me its name
but we're already onto something new

Each ocean wave distinct as a snowflake
each hair on our head given first name and last name

If it's *"from dust to dust"* it doesn't preclude
that our true home between is Elsewhere
and After

"Even between dusts our domain is ethereal"
saith Muriel

The Universe itself cube-shaped which is why
the Kaba in Mecca resonates so and doves are
incessantly circling above it

As one thing strikes another thing misses
here or elsewhere always and forever

Nothing disappears except disappearance
Nothing appears but appearance itself

If a mother giraffe kicks her shivering newborn
to stand up as soon as it's born in
spite of its wobbliness and start running in order to be
an inaccessible breakfast

then we need to decipher the kicks of love
from kicks of spite that may
seem to prevail

I'm sure the water's boiled by now
and the earth's again back to being round

The universe being as cubical as it is
whirls without making a sound

4/5

THE KNOT DONE AND UNDONE

Life is a death sentence

Death is a life sentence

                                4/12

AFTER I DIE

After I die
it will continue to rain and there will be that
comforting gurgle of water down the

drainpipe from the roof to the ground
and mist in the trees

After I die windows will still go up and
someone will lean out and shout
down to the street

Kitchens fill with the smell of garlic cooking
and school children screaming on playgrounds

After I die shadows will fall in deep
alleyways and the sun will sparkle
bridge spans and girders across
dazzling rivers the Walt Whitman the
Golden Gate all the

bridges in the world crossing some kind of
water even a rope bridge in the Amazon
navigated nimbly by a twenty-year old out on a
monkey hunt for his family

And huge waterfalls will roar
and people in hospitals suffer
with too many televisions

and in some places snowfall be
taller than houses

and in others drought crack the
earth to make it look like the
moon

And after I die everything will
still continue as if I were alive
but I won't be here to notice

and ants will continue to
hunt for morsels in my bathroom sink
owned by someone else

and some ants will find them and
some not and move on

4/12

OR EVEN MORE SO!

Dr. Doolittle the Jane Goodall of literature
spoke to animals and learned their secrets

in such a way as to help them beyond a
shot here or an overnight kennel there

They told him their life stories chatting amicably
and he went about single-mindedly
easing their hardships that Dr. Doolittle
he did

We have those scientists in the 60s who learned
The Secret Life of Plants by hooking electrodes to their leaves
and assessing their reactions even measuring some
excitement when their owners turned around from
many miles away and started home

The stars seem to speak to astrologers
and perhaps directly to astronauts though they may be
as they say loath to admit it

Maybe the earth by which I mean the
dirt itself very Adam's basic constituents
has spoken to an archeologist and said
"Dig here!" and lo! We have Troy or
Bonampak or Pompeii

Something's going on beyond our usual circumference

and only our receptor apparatuses need to be
sharpened to pick up its comprehensible noises

Did the deeps speak to Cousteau? Did those
ancient planets have a conversation with
Galileo? I'm sure Leonardo heard the
voices of the maelstrom the waterfall
and birds in flight

So may my nerves and meridians yell out to my
acupuncturist loud and clear God willing

just as clearly as you or me or
even more so!

4/13

PEACEFULLY SLEEPING REAPERS

Crossing the river Saint Christopher scratched his ear
and a mosquito became enlightened

Saint Theresa stepped on an ant that
hobbled home and delivered the good news

Hasan of Basra sat for a moment in the
shade in Basra and the sunlight
lamented and the shade rejoiced

The threads of light that travel our universe
from heart to heart are such that
if we adorned ourselves with only a
flicker of them the world would

sigh with relief and relax its tides and
tidal waves around us all

and that thing every child wishes for
blowing out birthday candles
might actually take place

and horses in their stalls whinny with delight
and moonlight through the high small

windows of barns slant down onto
peacefully sleeping reapers instead of the

fiery and fierce swingers of scythes
over the lamenting heads of the living

so longing for death

4/17

THE INVENTOR

Nefer Hotep invented the tweezers
but God invented the kidney
so who's the better inventor?

Johann Kirsten invented the thumbtack
but God invented the waterfall
so who's the better inventor?

Thomas Edison of course invented the light bulb
among other things such as the
phonograph the motion picture the incandescent filament
but God invented the wiggly antennae on ants
so who's the better inventor?

A glass for seeing far in the distance
but God invented the distance

A gyroscope for righting a ship's balance
but God invented balance

The guillotine that severs head from trunk
but God invented both head and trunk
(and intended them to go together)

And besides He gave the image of the padlock onto the
padlock-inventor's brain-screen in imagination
and each step toward successful completion
God also nudged or gave dream diagrams in the

night to all Eureka-shouting inventors

So in all of course He's inventor Number One
Source of the unending plethora of inventions
down to and including this poem
for which he has the true and sovereign copyright

but in His equally endless generosity
(to which I have no claim)

has kindly given it to me

4/18

WOULD JOY PERVADE US?

What if the machinery of time were just a
little motor somewhere like one of those

Erector Set motors behind a little curtain
near an open window on the third floor

whizzing a little as its gears turn and
everything that occupies any kind of space

grand small macrocosmic microcosmic
danced to its frail tune even those deep space

barely squintily visible planets and star clusters
where we have no idea at all when they

might break for lunch or lie down to die
and the machinery of time of course

never runs down nor speeds up nor
fluctuates in any way though we often

experience its intrepid doggedness at its
task as either swifter or slower and by

God's direct Power as sometimes altogether
non-existent though those gaps be rare and much

sought after among the clackety-clacks of
what we take as real life

And so here's this little machine after all
by flapping curtains on a wooden stool say

a really small machine of no imposing size
clickety-pinging along really modestly

and millennia of jungles lift their teaks
and crashes of ocean bash shore-rocks incessantly

And yet if this little contraption were to
short out or simply cease altogether

and go still maybe in a
worrisome puff of smoke and distinct

electrical odor then would all existence just
collapse or would as it were invisible

cage doors open to evocative melodious choir sound
and we'd flow out or in to some

timeless place on earth where things would
halt their progress towards decay

or would they? Or would we all simply
be expanded and ascended into a

sweet pure timelessness yet continuing to
breathe and breed as before or

would that curtained window there on the
third floor then be all there is?

4/23

THE TINIEST RABBI

> *"Written according to all the rabbinic scribal rules, these miniature scrolls are formally kosher and therefore suitable to be used for the liturgical Torah reading in the synagogue though in practice they were most likely too small to be read. The prayer book, published in Amsterdam in 1739, [is] ... a tiny volume the like of whose quality has never yet been seen, with delicate and diminutive characters together with new and beautiful vocalization, to teach the young how to keep the commandments."*
> (caption for exhibit of miniature texts)

1

I am a very small rabbi the smallest in my family
so small in fact my father put me in his pocket to go to synagogue
every morning and evening to pray and I still remember the
smell of his rough wool in the dark corner of his coat and I would
stand up to look out as we passed the shops and he greeted the
shopkeepers selling hides and herbs and piles of chickpeas spices
and
the booksellers…

Ah the booksellers! my favorites
with their thick spectacles and black beards
bent over books piled all around them extending back into the
blackness of their shops shelves upon shelves of volumes carefully
handwritten in black letters bound in
sweetly odoriferous leathers

2

There are more of us than you might think
not just little but really very little in fact
standing in our stocking feet about
as tall as pigeons

We live a precarious existence but as I've gotten older I see
we don't live any more precarious existence than anyone else
and may be even more blessed than most people
for we stand guard over precious things when
night's lamps are extinguished

We stand guard over God's
implements of scholarship pens and quills and
fine sand for drying though we're
no angels

Some say imps others elves some sprites but we're really
human through and through

Our jobs on earth unnoticed which is
actually our preference after all

Anonymity our badge of honor

Doing God's work almost invisibly while the big world
booms all around us

our source of humble pride

3

I wondered growing up what on earth I might do at my size

though I'd spend my days in nature visiting plants in our
family garden tending growing things since I could
hear their sighs and soft songs more clearly because of my
kinship with subtle shifts and aching energies of all small things

As well as animals squirrels and rodents
some benign some rapacious
some even terrifying which in fact is what

made me think I should concentrate on
more indoor pursuits and cultivate
more scholarly aptitudes

(and this part could also be entitled: *The Rat that Nearly Ate Me*)

4

I felt on a par with ants in their restless treks
smudges on windows when the sun hits them
shadows of everything but especially the
glitter of snow since it seems to come
from a center of light almost inaccessible in this world
but funneled if you will from the Next
that mysterious Other World invisible to our eyes
mankind and womankind seem
bent on understanding with their

texts and rigorous labors though they
don't often admit it

Writing took on a wonderful magnetism for me
It seemed to be a place I could almost inhabit
Hebrew letters like little corrals little rooms with their
four squarish walls built up from earthly horizons or
dangling from celestial horizontals

And I moved at ease in these rooms with their thick black strokes
on vellum

I mean I began to find my size fit in with the hand calligraphed
texts

I breathed easily inside these walls and
flowed out through their openings

5

How do we find our calling? No matter what size?
Why does one man kiss and another kill
one woman ride a coach with a bonnet of feathers and bodice of
lace and another wash clothes on the riverbank
with her calloused feet?

I hearkened
That's all I can say
And God talked

A void began to fill up in me
an echo place that was also a mercury mirror upon which
letters formed and black pen strokes flashed against white
and gold lettering bubbled and carefully curved

But I was this tiny rabbi this most rabbity rabbi
small-faced and tiny pawed with fingers like wiry filaments
more worthy of riding in my father's pocket than
having a calling

Or so I assumed

6

"Not so!" my father boomed
(he always boomed it seemed with his divine voice)

"Nothing is overlooked in this universe
neither gnat nor snowflake sunbeam nor avalanche

Nothing has a meaningless purpose"

So I undertook to listen more intently to God's Voice telling me
whatever threading alleyway to glory He might indicate

Whatever highway over whatever hills into whatever
sunrise

7

One day I found myself sinking into a huge text
with words almost as big as my head

I sank into their resonating rooms of sound and meaning
a purple maelstrom winding down and up at the
same time past higher earths and even higher heavens
each with a clear musical tone and numerical equivalent and
heading toward a holy light I'd seen only once at my
birth that haunted my days

A *Yes!* that came with my soul

So I took up a sliver and
dipped it in an inkwell on my father's desk and made
letters one after another stroke after stroke
down and curved up and straight until I was writing
things out of myself I'd heard and learned in synagogue
and repeated in the corner of my father's pocket only now

I made page after page with letters I could read and recite
holding them in my hands

And as I wrote the light grew greater
God's Light spread in my being making me both
infinite and infinitesimal until I was almost a
vanished thing altogether not
knowing if I'd expanded past mortal limits or contracted into
almost utter annihilation

Which seems the finest stance before God's Holy Light after all
for that Light to fall with its full strength
through the world

And my dear father found the tiny pages I'd written
and he smiled and stroked his beard and held them up to the light
and squinted through his now tear-filled eyes

and I became micro-calligrapher for God
maker of scrolls and books for the tiny the nearsighted and children

or to simply hold a miraculous thing and know the perfectly
written reams of words inside are

magnificent reverberations of wonder

8

And the original Tree contained in its apex the root and in its root
the apex

And rainbows from within Divine Charge in a bundle
extended their lashes through the seventy thousand
worlds

And the worlds trembled to hear those lashes
and in their desire to stand up took shape and form
out of coagulant darkness

And the darkness split into atomic structures dormant until

the True Tree's light animated their hairs and
enlivened their passageways
leading to original Adam who was now the human Tree of origin
his root his apex and his apex his root
and in his longing for reflective moonlight his chest opened
and his solar heart expanded taking the
shape of his opposite nature
and Eve was born

And bells rang and wood creaked in the
forest and waves lapped shores around
human-shaped continents whose reality was articulated by

the shimmer of letters pouring from the mouth of space as
sound captured in God's personal alphabets
whose Words became the material world and whose
meanings are the spirit world unchanging throughout time
though all things be in flux

except change itself which remains constant forever

amen

4/25

(*Written by invitation for* The Chosen: Philadelphia's
Great Hebraica Exhibit *at the Rosenbach Museum,
and read there with other invited poets in conjunction
with the exhibit*)

NOT FINISHED BUT ABANDONED

The hanging vine named Helen or Hector
and the hornet waiting to be tossed out of a Styrofoam cup

and the faucets holding their water
and the cats anticipating can-opener music

and the whisper whisper of the hot water heater's pilot light
and the telephones mute at 4 A.M.

and the clock hands moving intrepidly forward
and earnestly trying to multiply myself by zero before Allah

and the windows now empty of images
blacked over as if against the enemy

when the enemy's sitting here writing this poem
to the coiling snake inside who turns seraphic after I'm dead

as well as invisible listeners and readers
and the cat now coming downstairs to beg for food

and night stretching to infinity on both sides as well as
above and below

and the things left to do and
the things done

and this poem not finished
but abandoned

4/27

OUR CHILDREN

The children that we have become the
teachers who will break us into bits

Our staunch confrontations with the world
pulverized or tested

Back across the bent backs of our parents
and ancestors

as if all the generations were tied to a dock
waiting for us to skip rocks across their bows

in the arctic with floating ice-chunks
or the tropics with its malarial fevers

Our children who take from us
cues for eye-winks or mouth-frowns

challenging the very blood that
courses through them to stand at the

crossroads and march on as the world's
train whistles shriek shrill beside them

And we're covered in the mist of passage
as they pass

tossing us a look or two
in passing

God keep them in their groove
for every day's tomorrow

O Prophet press them in your praise

4/29

HEARTBEAT

God put a heartbeat in every one of us

Isn't that proof enough?

4/29

HIS REALITY IN ALL THINGS

Each fiber and entwined filament of the universe
originates in His light and culminates
in the fully lit person on earth of the Prophet Muhammad

Each energy roaring or silent through all created things
has his noble face and
streams naked through space repeating his blessed name

Each atom in our beings from here to Timbuktu
falls into place within the
bliss of his consciousness and is enlivened there

The very air vibrates with his remembrance
and longs to return to his initial starting place in a
circle that has no end or beginning

Each sea wave faces his face and
shouts for joy in the *shush* of its whisperings

The high pitched sound that thrums through the
world is his pure heartbeat resounding

Known or unbeknownst to us
there's always perfect recognition of Ahmad
the beloved one
in each encounter and departure of ours

world without end

Amen

BRIGHTER THAN DAY

The body is rolled in

"It can't be mine" I say
*"I fit into it so nicely you can't
even tell"*

Looking down it lies so peacefully
but from this angle it's unrecognizable as me

Nothing moves
Mine is all movement
even when asleep

No context
Mine is always in a context
the bed living room the Grand Canyon
standing on a rock for a photograph at
fifteen a 3D photo my father took
like an eagle with backdrop falling away
behind me

This inert colorless slug
it can't be me

"Take another look" I'm told
Nothing looks familiar eyes closed mouth
clamped shut breathless and still

Indeterminate age from this perspective

now that I've joined the ancients
and futurists everpresently awake

"Looks like it couldn't lift a finger"
I say and it's true

"Like a work of art" I say
but not a terribly successful one
stretched out like that with no
expression on its face woodenly inert

I'm shimmering
It looks like clay

I'm weightless
It looks heavily laden

"It's yours" they say
"Okay" I say since there's no
other around even
close to what I feel now as it

begins to fade away
and I'm in a landscape that's

brighter than day

5/4

THE BOOK OF UNCOMMON BEAUTY

The book of uncommon beauty floats
down in front of me and lands

open on my knee

The book of common beauty also floats
no less slowly and lands on my

other knee

Spirits keep rising from their deep
vellum pages and somersaulting

through the air landing in each other's
places in such a way that I can

see what is written and depicted on the
pages in exquisite mineral colors

all the way through from cover to cover

It rains incessantly onto the book of
common beauty but never

wets the pages

A sure and prismatically separated
light shines out from the

book of uncommon beauty

Etherial beasts keep rising through the
pages of the book of uncommon beauty

and they display themselves before me on a
horizon that seems to extend to infinity

Large lumbering creatures who
look at me

Lithe quick beings more reptilian
seem to almost pirouette in front of me

Then scamper off into the bush I hadn't
noticed grows on either side of me

A flame of light appears above both
books in the air and out of it steps

a man and a maiden clad in the
garments of Eden singing a wordless song

and they come forward and each takes
up in one graceful swoop one of these

books and flees away down invisible
lanes in front of me without

turning one glance again towards me

And I am left here with an empty place
now on each knee

But one tiny mammal with huge eyes
runs across and hides under one knee

to show me it is more than mere
reverie

> 5/11

CRIME NOVEL

Let's see —
A perfectly crafted crime novel

A perfect anapestic poem each stanza
clipped to a "T"

A perfect pot thrown on a wheel and
perfect within millimeters on each side

A perfect arch through which the perfectly
tended garden is framed for one
perfect moment as you approach

A perfectly geometrical building topped by
a perfect dome as if suspended by angels

All this perfection aching toward something
unachievable but echoed in the attempt

as if we all leapt at the moon like Li Po
hoping to embrace it or become at least
its absolute whiteness

The perfect building crumbled by time
the perfect garden overrun by equally
perfect weeds and the arch perfectly toppled down

The perfect pot knocked over by panthers or

sent flying in a rage against the
perfect inlaid wall

And both poem and novel unread and
forgotten

until it all begins again as dependable as
breath

We climb towards perfection eyes ablaze
not knowing that He Who is Perfect and
Perfection itself has put it in our

hearts to yearn so for perfection

Our lives the perfect crime we're meant to unravel

toward the one perfect solution

5/11

ESPECIALLY AND MOST PARTICULARLY

Especially and most particularly
the gown of stars the beloved wears
stretched across the sky

Then most emphatically the shadow of the
huge boat cast against dolphin crowded seas
at midnight
and that boat is death

Most of all the endless blue both in the
ocean's deep and out into space until His Voice
takes over with its soothing Majesty
speaking in silence of elementally secret things

Sluices and causeways bridges and tall
trees growing in isolation since the
dawn of the world poking through
heaven

Cataracts and natural disasters enumerated
and recorded with each cry and prayer
to be played back from its actual
situation in the Unseen on the
Day of Resurrection and not before

All these God's calling cards and He calls on us
and doesn't stop calling us to Him
past radio blare by means of a dawn bird's

poignant burble in the dark in
sibilant repetition out there
over and over

And the heart gets up in the place it's in
and strides forth without moving into
expanding circles of sweet delirium to
face that Voice and listen to
that Face simmer down through its

heartbeating bone

For there's no response equal to the call
but no response is
no response at all

and the crystal mirror that
shines on the sea floor
has our perfect reflection in it
from even

before the call

5/12

RIPPLING RACE HORSE

A rippling race horse stands in the glistening sun
its undulant muscles like lithe ropes
pulled up around a sleek machine
its classical head come alive as
impassive and Stoic as late night silence itself
its great soft eyes almost pitying
as it gazes out of ancient animal lineage
onto the simplistic affairs of human greed

Inside its legs wild horses run across
Mongolian horizons under huge cloud skies
like match flames held from right to left
lighting up pitch blackness with shattering fire

And holds its head high on a noble neck as
weather-stormed as the Trojan horse full of
crouched warriors tightlipped waiting for the
right time to strike

And shifts its weight to other feet
hooves shoed with adamant hardness
that will soon beat indelible patterns
on a track that rotates as the earth turns

around a more stationary and fiery center

5/14

THE METAPHYSICS OF EXCRETION

If instead of what we do excrete
God had somehow fashioned us to expel
our waste as slim globes of glass that would be
gathered every few days and pounded back into
powder

Or a gauzy odorless tissue like ribbony strips that
totally evaporate upon contact with air

But the mystery is that every
potentate must poop every pope poop down to
every pooping pauper the most
ruthless tyrant must excuse himself
and the most blood-thirsty madman stop to relieve himself
enwreathed for some moments in less
pleasant biological atmospheres of his or
her internal making after caviar or

corn bread venison or grub our alchemical
combustion engine burning and extracting
the nutritious elixirs as all things in creation seem to do
leaving waste somewhere right in the
midst as birds do or behind bushes as perhaps
Adam and Eve did either before or after
the great divulgement that

encased us forever in the metaphysics of our shuddering flesh

our spirits finally excreting our bodies as well
lifting off from their rotting offal left behind

into purer and more congenial
latitudes

5/16

THE BAREST HANDHOLD

I don't even know what I know
much less what I don't know

A Chinese laundry full of coats and shirts
knows more than I know

Boats at sea heading toward a faint light in fog
have a better idea than I do
and get there with more grit and determination

The night seems to have fallen onto the
earth like black velvet yardage
fold after fold thicker than the sea-bottom
where fangs with fins pass at the
slightest incandescence with jaws agape

Heartbeat after heartbeat taps it out
as if with the barest handhold on a sheer
side of rock with the

whole world falling away below us

Only God can help us in such a state
His Prophet the woolly sherpa up ahead
face into the blizzard peace be upon him

and the canyon's echoes ringing with his name

5/19

ROTATION ENOUGH

Spend a ripe drop to a whole
river fill

A live breath to make the sky shake

A long road take to make short life's
unrolling firm

A sigh in the heart to let the wind in

Leave off what's left when the whole
world lifts its shade
and let your wild sunlight spread
a place where all may live

No planet can bequeath what you
may give in a short wink

Though you do not spin a grand orbit
your turning has rotation
enough to win

5/24

EVENTUALLY

Eventually the creation of rivers of
emeralds and topazes became old
and they liquefied into limpid glittering
water runs heading to the sea

which turned liquid as well after
millennia as gigantic jellyfish crooning
incessantly at the moon having consumed
in their gourmet way from whales to
minnows those unfortunate enough to have
crossed their path and entered their
insatiable maws

Trees of ivory and gold got old and turned to
wood and leaves a wind could
bend and rustle

And earth itself once a gigantic diamond
turning on its axis for all to see against the
black velvet display of space crumbled to dirt
except for a few perfect shards now
embedded in its earthy bowels
for deep South Africans to find as they
sing their songs

And all of us as well on a good day
might reveal in a certain light our more

resplendent perfect original selves
made of powder and radiance
flowing gold arterial blood and
corridor minds opening to central
chambers of such architectural magnificence

greedy potentates for the riches of this world
would faint away amazed at stellar domes and our
elementally elegant latticework letting in

the intense divine singing of the stars
burning in their appointed places in space
with the same dazzling light that burns
eternally in our hearts

5/25

MEMENTO MORI

At the thought of death the constable shivers
in his little constabulary kiosk

The cook cracks an egg into the quiche
feeling a spine-tingle that jiggles the mix

And even astronomy itself beyond our affable atmosphere
orbiting us like another conked moon
gets an icy perspiration whose cold beads
immediately float in the air like pearls of snow

It's a goofy proposition all around and even
I'm a bit uncomfortable sitting here cool as a
rutabaga in a rutabaga bed contemplating its
effect on others holding it all literally at
crook'd arm's length
the pen at the end of this hand just as
easily writing out a death certificate as this
juicy little poem instead

That stoppage of breath past the
edge of no return
and once dead the tickets to the theater are
invalid being non-transferable except on a
rare Tuesday if the clerk's compassionate

And merry-go-round calliope music
takes on a suddenly rather sinister quality

And romping white tigers in the zoo with their
bright orange plastic barrel have an even more
ethereal whiteness that's at odds with their
very terrestrial tigerness

which is what death is all about
the *not-life not-breath not-another-heartbeat*
place inhabited exclusively by the dead

on their deserted island
in the middle of our conceptual nothingness
utterly oblivious to our grieved wrenchings
with far more than those of us left behind
to preoccupy themselves with

seeing now every hair and flinch of action or
inaction's innermost intended meaning displayed on the
big screen that stretches from Eternity's pole to pole

The same one all orbiting planets swim in
except that His pure Voice is its ocean of
sound and His Name is the tone of it

as it all goes around

5/26

TOO DELIRIOUS

*"If you're too delirious to continue
that should be enough for achievement*

if your delirium is out of love not madness"

he said spinning slightly around on one foot
with roses blooming all along his arms
and his face now a lot like a giraffe's

with those huge sweet eyes on the verge of
tears and those eyelashes like multiple

black crescent moons sweeping
across them

The road turned golden at that and the
trees on either side started chanting salutations

Even the sky overhead became an upside-down
mirror for a second in which this

dreary world became inverted but looked
more like a garden than a place of

worry and devastation misplaced anger and
senseless killing

Here was a phrase that soaked up all the

bad we might be so willing to manifest

and in a matter of seconds turned it through the
entire larval stages from embryonic dot to
busting through cocoon walls

to the slow stretched-out ignited flight of a thousand white
butterflies of our inherent good nature

on strong wings
toward the sun

5/29

SEE!

Each drop in the splatter of a color splash

Each part of a curve in the arc of an
infinite spiral

Each reverberation on its way somewhere
from a light beam directed outward

Each stuttered part of a sentence by a
lover too shy to confess his love

Each ant's footprint in the great trek
across the white frosting of a birthday cake

Each momentary high point in a nearly
shipwrecked schooner's plunge on the
breakers of tornado seas

calls out for completion in the Eye of Unity
and simultaneously contains both the
whole of which it's a part in a

divine totality and a fulfillment in
itself of the body's purpose of which it is

seemingly just an annoying fragment uncoordinated with the
rest of the flexion or relaxation or
impetus toward lurch or toward

lax shrinkage away from its aim

And we see with a pried-open eye
the little scallops of light all created actions make

above the surface of the literally placid
silvery lake of God's peace that stretches from
one infinity to another in the

eternal wink that lasts a lifetime
gone from the beginning

into His pool of such light no
darkness of any kind escapes from it
and has barely begun or is in fact

see! nearly over before it's begun

Only Allah
at all moments

in His total Oneness

In His total Oneness

Present

at all moments

ALL THE GREAT HISTORICAL FIGURES

All the great historical figures found they were
taking the same subway since
they were already underground

Caesar's and the senators' blood-stained
togas nearly got stuck in the doors

Joan of Arc came in and sat down holding her
carbonized stake the way a child holds a
teddy bear

But what was astonishing was the number of
historical figures none of us knew anything about

The great Aztec astronomer the great Incan
visionary priest the Inuit shaman

The Aboriginal prophet the saint from
Tierra del Fuego who performed ten verified miracles

The village silversmith from Bhutan
the first ever orchestra conductor from Madagascar

The train plunges underground but stops at
none of the usual stations

None of the passengers notice each other
and none say a word

None are let out but new ones are
constantly let in

as it plunges on deep in
diluvial silence

                                                                                              6/4

MAN IN A TREE

A man sat in a tree and counted his
fingers and toes

and always came up with twenty

Was he statesman or shaman?
(A mirror there showed his face while shaving

so he was no shaman nor
louche mathematician

wild magician
nor bohemian musician)

Though he did hum as he did his sum
which always came up with twenty

as he sat in a tree

I've thrown caution to the winds
with no idea why this man this tree and his

twenty perfect digits at this time are

of any importance
to the way the world

comes to its sad culminations and

disastrous conclusions time after time

with folk only seeming to
just learn from their mistakes

how better to
repeat them

                 6/6

BOOMERANG

There's a poem like a boomerang
that goes from continent to continent and from
language to language and yet comes
back to its original tosser

It whistles through the air end over end side over
side *Oh!* and its melody makes the

sunshine squeak and sea waves clap their
zillion watery hands to a white foam

Original tosser stand among us
to let us all hear and understand
the poem that links us

and let no cave dweller lurk too far
back in the shadows nor no high roller

feel rich beyond your propelling need to
sing out through every word known to us

the song of your original boomerang
toss into the air

that lifts us beyond us

6/8

DEATHBED MOMENT

O deathbed moment of death or
death standing in space at the appointed hour or
minute or death by drowning or a lingering
death by inches over time however the
appointment and I know I'm talking to

the Angel of Death here or really talking to
God direct Who's the only True Knower of this
most precious event held in velvets and wrapped in
starry linen in a cloudless portion of
space somewhere waiting to be

put into service or installed directly into my
own space-time continuum kept from then on from
mortally continuing

O you then *whomever* but really *me* then
(the only one needing to listen) no way

truly to prepare not like Rimbaud's
mother or Sarah Bernhardt by lying in
dug graves or padded coffins to get the
impossible "feel" of the place

nor even perhaps by speculation like
figuring out a detective novel exactly

when where and *how* and being alertly ready for

any contingency no matter how intricately

strange like falling off a giraffe or being
run over by stampeding buffalo in

someplace unknown and at this moment
we're not even desiring to be visiting

Yet after all our meeting is assured and as
inevitable as this poem's last word

not yearned for as much as thought about
though we may yearn for the meeting with our

Beloved Lord His date made especially for us and
perfectly prepared

Red sunlight on a blue sea

Sphinx opening its eyes

Elevator going infinitely and simultaneously
upward and downward

A rowing toward no shore

Opening a box that is ourselves finding
at last valued treasure at its

true value

Smoke that becomes substance

Kiss of God deliberate through the ages

Meadow of real flowers

Happy action at last

come home

                                                                    6/10

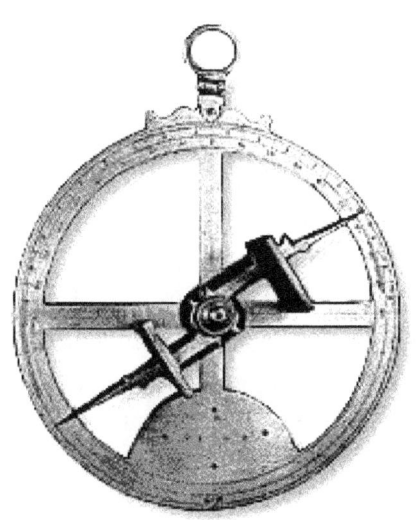

ABOUT THE AUTHOR

Born in 1940 in Oakland, California, Daniel Abdal-Hayy Moore's first book of poems, *Dawn Visions*, was published by Lawrence Ferlinghetti of City Lights Books, San Francisco, in 1964, and the second in 1972, *Burnt Heart/Ode to the War Dead*. He created and directed *The Floating Lotus Magic Opera Company* in Berkeley, California in the late 60s, and presented two major productions, *The Walls Are Running Blood*, and *Bliss Apocalypse*. He became a Sufi Muslim in 1970, performed the Hajj in 1972, and lived and traveled throughout Morocco, Spain, Algeria and Nigeria, landing in California and publishing *The Desert is the Only Way Out*, and *Chronicles of Akhira* in the early 80s (Zilzal Press). Residing in Philadelphia since 1990, in 1996 he published *The Ramadan Sonnets* (Jusoor/City Lights), and in 2002, *The Blind Beekeeper* (Jusoor/Syracuse University Press). He has been the major editor for a number of works, including *The Burdah* of Shaykh Busiri, translated by Shaykh Hamza Yusuf, and the poetry of Palestinian poet, Mahmoud Darwish, translated by Munir Akash. He is also widely published on the worldwide web: *The American Muslim*, *DeenPort*, and his own website and poetry blog, among others: www.danielmoorepoetry.com, www.ecstaticxchange.wordpress.com. He has been the poetry editor for *Islamica Magazine* and *Seasons Journal*, and a new translation by Munir Akash of *State of Siege*, by Mahmoud Darwish, from Syracuse University Press. The Ecstatic Exchange Series is bringing out the extensive body of his works of poetry (a complete list of published works on page 2).

POETIC WORKS by Daniel Abdal-Hayy Moore

Dawn Visions (Published by City Lights, 1964)
Burnt Heart/Ode to the War Dead (Published by City Lights, 1972)
This Body of Black Light Gone Through the Diamond (Printed by Fred Stone, Cambridge, Mass, 1965)
On The Streets at Night Alone (1965?)
All Hail the Surgical Lamp (1967)
States of Amazement (1970)

Abdallah Jones and the Disappearing-Dust Caper (published by The Ecstatic Exchange/Crescent Series, 2006)
'Ala ud-Deen and the Magic Lamp
The Chronicles of Akhira (1981) (published by Zilzal Press with Typoglyphs by Karl Kempton, 1986)
Mouloud (1984) (A Zilzal Press chapbook, 1995)
Man is the Crown of Creation (1984)
The Look of the Lion (The Parabolas of Sight) (1984)
The Desert is the Only Way Out (completed 4/21/84) (Zilzal Press chapbook, 1985)
Atomic Dance (1984) (am here books, 1988)
Outlandish Tales (1984)
Awake as Never Before (12/26/84) (Zilzal Press chapbook, 1993)
Glorious Intervals (1/1/85) (Zilzal Press chapbook, ?)
Long Days on Earth/Book I (1/28 – 4/22/85)
Long Days on Earth/Book II (Hayy Ibn Yaqzan)(end 7/26/85)
Long Days on Earth/Book III (1/22/86)
Long Days on Earth/Book IV (1986)
The Ramadan Sonnets (Long Days on Earth/Book V) (5/9 – 6/11/86) (Published by Jusoor/City Lights Books, 1996) (Republished as Ramadan Sonnets by The Ecstatic Exchange, 2005)
Long Days on Earth/Book VI (6-8/30/86)
Holograms (9/4/86 – 3/26/87)
History of the World (The Epic of Man's Survival) (4/7 – 6/18/87)
Exploratory Odes (6/25 – 10/18/87)
The Man at the End of the World (11/11 – 12/10/87)
The Perfect Orchestra (3/30 – 7/25/88) (Published by The Ecstatic Exchange, 2009)

Fed from Underground Springs (7/30 – 11/23/88)
Ideas of the Heart (11/27/88 – 5/5/89)
New Poems (scattered poems, out of series, from 3/24 – 8/9/89)
Facing Mecca (5/16 – 11/11/89)
A Maddening Disregard for the Passage of Time (11/17/89 – 5/20/90) (Published by The Ecstatic Exchange, 2009)
The Heart Falls in Love with Visions of Perfection (6/15/90 – 6/2/91)
Like When You Wave at a Train and the Train Hoots Back at You (Farid's Book) (6/11 – 7/26/91) (Published by The Ecstatic Exchange, 2008)
Orpheus Meets Morpheus (8/1/91– 3/14/92)
The Puzzle (3/21/92 – 8/17/93)
The Greater Vehicle (10/17/93 – 4/30/94)
A Hundred Little 3-D Pictures (5/14/94 – 9/11/95)
The Angel Broadcast (9/29 – 12/17/95)
Mecca/Medina Time-Warp (12/19/95 – 1/6/96) (Published as a Zilzal Press chapbook, 1996, included in Sparrow on the Prophet's Tomb, published by The Ecstatic Exchange, 2009)
Miracle Songs for the Millennium (1/20 – 10/16/96)
The Blind Beekeeper (11/15/96 – 5/30/97) (Published 2002 by Jusoor/Syracuse University Press)
Chants for the Beauty Feast (6/3 – 10/28/97)
You Open a Door and it's a Starry Night (10/29/97 – 5/23/98) (Published by The Ecstatic Exchange, 2009)
Salt Prayers (5/29 – 10/24/98) (Published by The Ecstatic Exchange, 2005)
Some (10/25/98 – 4/25/99)
Flight to Egypt (5/1 – 5/16/99)
I Imagine a Lion (5/21 – 11/15/99) (Published by The Ecstatic Exchange, 2006)
Millennial Prognostications (11/25/99 – 2/2/2000) (Published by the Ecstatic Exchange, 2009)
Shaking the Quicksilver Pool (2/4 – 10/8/2000) (Published by The Ecstatic Exchange, 2009)
Blood Songs (10/9/2000 – 4/3/2001)
The Music Space (4/10 – 9/16/2001) (Published by The Ecstatic Exchange, 2007)
Where Death Goes (9/20/2001 – 5/1/2002) (Published by The Ecstatic Exchange, 2009)
The Flame of Transformation Turns to Light (99 Ghazals Written in English) (5/14 – 8/21/2002) (Published by The Ecstatic Exchange, 2007)

Through Rose-Colored Glasses (7/22/2002 – 1/15/2003) (Published by The Ecstatic Exchange, 2007)
Psalms for the Broken-Hearted (1/22 – 5/25/2003) (Published by The Ecstatic Exchange, 2006)
Hoopoe's Argument (5/27 – 9/18/03)
Love is a Letter Burning in a High Wind (9/21 – 11/6/2003) (Published by The Ecstatic Exchange, 2006)
Laughing Buddha/Weeping Sufi (11/7/2003 – 1/10/2004) (Published by The Ecstatic Exchange, 2005)
Mars and Beyond (1/20 – 3/29/2004) (Published by The Ecstatic Exchange, 2005)
Underwater Galaxies (4/5 – 7/21/2004) (Published by The Ecstatic Exchange, 2007)
Cooked Oranges (7/23/2004 – 1/24/2005 (Published by The Ecstatic Exchange, 2007)
Holiday from the Perfect Crime (1/25 – 6/11/2005)
Stories Too Fiery to Sing Too Watery to Whisper (6/13 – 10/24/2005)
Coattails of the Saint (10/26/2005 – 5/10/2006) (Published by The Ecstatic Exchange, 2006)
In the Realm of Neither (5/14/2006 – 11/12/06) (Published by The Ecstatic Exchange, 2008)
Invention of the Wheel (11/13/06 – 6/10/07) (Published by The Ecstatic Exchange, 2010)
The Sound of Geese Over the House (6/15 – 11/4/07)
The Fire Eater's Lunchbreak (11/11/07 – 5/19/2008) (Published by The Ecstatic Exchange, 2008)
Sparks Off the Main Strike (5/24/2008 – 1/10/2009)
Stretched Out on Amethysts (1/13 – 9/17/2009) (Published by The Ecstatic Exchange, 2010)
The Throne Perpendicular to All that is Horizontal (9/18/09 – 1/25/10)
In Constant Incandescence (2/10/10 –)

www.ingramcontent.com/pod-product-compliance
Lightning Source LLC
Chambersburg PA
CBHW020903090426
42736CB00008B/477